YOU MIGHT FEEL THIS
A Poetry Collection

BY
William Thomas Brumley

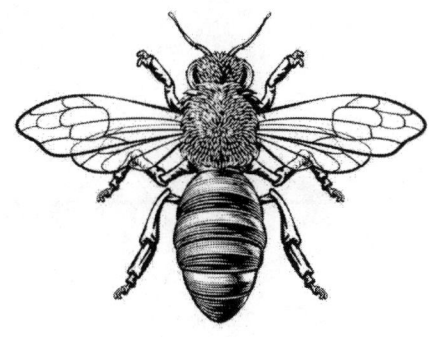

You Might Feel This BY William Thomas Brumley

Copyright ©2021 William Thomas Brumley

All rights reserved. No portion of this book may be reproduced in any form without permission from the publisher, except as permitted by U.S. copyright law. For permissions contact: WTBPoetry@outlook.com

INTRODUCTION

With my first poetry collection, I did not want to over-edit and polish true emotion. I want my words and feelings to translate off the page from when I was writing. I did not want to overthink it. I want my words and feelings to convey naturally. Poetry should not be overly polished. Write what you're feeling in the moment. Do not get bogged down in trying to perfect it. You are what you feel.

That is what the following blank pages are for. Write and draw how you feel. The decision lies in your hands alone. Share this book with others if you wish. Write amazing poetry you'd love to share with the world. I want to change the world with our words. Our words can make a difference.

As someone who suffers from crippling anxiety. I know writing emotions can help you get a better handle on how you are feeling. Since I started writing poetry, I discovered it is a good way to vent when you have no one else to talk to, or anyone that understands.

I want this collection to help you feel something. It might even awaken the poet inside you. I want it to help you through a difficult time you may be enduring. Keep being who you are. Write the next great poem. If you are an artist, draw an amazing picture. These blank pages are your typewriter and your canvas.

Thank you for giving this collection a chance. I hope you enjoy it.

-William Thomas Brumley

YOU MIGHT FEEL THIS

A
Poetry Collection

WTB Poetry

I wanted to dedicate this collection to Emily Dickinson, my inspiration to write poetry.

Photo credit Amherst College Archives & Special Collections

I DWELL IN POSSIBILITY
-Emily Dickinson

Bee's Sting

The bees sting was not as painful as your words and your absence
The words to say cannot be found
They have been locked away
I yearn to hear the sweet truths from your angelic voice
Please, speak to me say anything
Words that will calm and soothe me
From this torment of restrictions bestowed upon my happiness

Familiar Friend

The ground has split in two
I tread lightly over the divide
Monitoring every single step
fears have come back to haunt me
Ones that invade every corner of my brain
Fear is an old familiar friend of whom I've fallen out of touch with
Why does this shape haunt me?
Can they not find another for torment?
To be the chosen of their intent is a curse
A curse for which I can not break

Your thoughts here

Ghost Carriage

The past is gone and far away
Only accessible by a ghost carriage
Grab hold of me, hang on tight
For I can not promise what happens next
Lines in the sky
Lines in the sand
A new path for which I cannot cross
Why would I want to?
For here I am comfortable
For here I am safe
Where are you?
Are you safe too?
My hand is here to extend
Reach out for me
I'll reach for you too
The two of us safe
Two of us lost in bliss
I forgive you
Will you forgive me?

Your thoughts here

River's Compass

For I am not lost. The stars gaze upon me. The moon has cast its pale glow and embraced me. For the grass on my feet is my guide. The dirt upon the trail is a map to my chambers
The rushing sound of the flowing river is my compass
For this narrow path, I stumble
Nothing could hurt me more
I've lost all faith in direction
No signs to guide me further
Now The stars have burned away
The moon has faded into oblivion
Everything faded to a never-ending darkness.
The ground finally gives way
I am now alone

Your thoughts here

Counted Stars

Counting the stars until a new thought invaded my brain
and pushed away the simple pleasures I was embracing
Pain etched into my memory
Far deeper than any pleasant dream
Staring at the sky I feel nothing
But only for a moment
For I can no longer grasp eternity
The sense of impending fulfillment
Draws near and is closer than it has has ever been
Such a powerful sensation on a exuberant scale
I shall make this last forever
For this is the greatest feeling I can ever remember

Your thoughts here

Hopes' Weeping Veil

Hope is a weeping veil
For I have seen one
It was worn by a man
A man on the decrepit bridge
That I have always been scared to journey
Will he to dance to the cries of
fragmented fantasies?
For the world spins
And I am not a willing passenger

Your thoughts here

Melancholy's Maestro

The piano's keys no longer make music
Your heart no longer beats with melody
The presence of you has strayed from here
A presence on the hill calls your name
It satiates my desire to hear your sobriquet
Melancholy has returned to me in your absence
The Sun recovers from its escape from the far horizon
Staring into the bright star I wish for its demise
A black hole that will swallow the world and my sorrows
The modern burning catastrophe played by an orchestra
Without a maestro.
A beautiful canvas never to be finished without its painter
My eyes will forever be robbed of their color

Your thoughts here

Tiny White Dot

For this pill is a chariot
To take me away from pain
It gives me such euphoria
I hear yelling but I feel nothing
Slight discomfort does not arise
One more dose is simply too many
For all I need is in front of me
We have become one in serenity

Your thoughts here

Blue Dress

The blue dress is what I noticed most
For the one who wears it knows the truth
An impossible beautiful truth
The color begins to fade
Distancing itself from the pain of the wearer
It begins to assemble a makeshift kite
One of a beautiful blue and green
I grab hold of its string, for it is my lifeline
It shall pull me into a new life
Into a new direction, onto the unseen path

YOU MIGHT FEEL THIS

Your thoughts here

The Grand Gesture

The grand gesture summons me to the depths
I know it well, for it is death
Whom is an acquaintance of mine
For him, we should not fear
For he is the only one who shall steer
Us through the darkest night
A neverending unstoppable night
Winter chills me to thy bones
My feet frozen to the ground
As they are in time
I feel the snow hit my face
It melts into my warm skin
I tend to think of my love
My love for memories passed
For memories to be had
For the time that melts away as the snow
How much time do I have left
What shall be left of me when I am dead and gone
I ponder the lives that have faded to dust under thy feet
Where will you go I ask myself
There is no answer
There never was
Please forgive me
I know nothing of time, I know nothing at all
I only know how to love thee

YOU MIGHT FEEL THIS

Your thoughts here

Ghost Ship

Wind, terrible wind
I long to see the shores again
Stuck in this empty but so alive sea
The waves rise and scream as they pine
For our mighty vessel to join them at the bottom of it's depths
The dark and empty abyss
For which I cannot see
The most beautiful sound of the siren calls to us
The succubus has already taken men from this mighty ship
I for one no longer know how long I can resist
I scream, I scream. But nothing
I need to touch the land again
I need to see you. Why did we leave?
A foolish expedition by foolish men
An adventure with no reward to be reaped
The only one who will ever see what is embodied on this vessel
Are the ghost ships that lay as tombs
Now and forever lost to the depths
Far. Far down

Your thoughts here

Seclusion

In seclusion, I exist
Pixelated foundation
Crumbling under the pressure
For to exist is seclusion
The isolation can be defining
Lack of sound is my blanket
For the negativity cannot drain away the hope
The absence of light forces me to feel around in
the dark for the touch of appreciation

YOU MIGHT FEEL THIS

The Grand Scheme

Why has this scheme occupied and consumed me?
It is unforgiving and it taunts me in the night
Escape is not feasible nor is surrender
My chambers have become cold and empty
For one thing, is perfect it is the light
It no longer shines through my window
The shudders of time have closed
I try to pry them open but they are not forgiving
They budge but slam shut and shatter
Shatter into a thousand pieces
This gives me hope for a glimpse of illumination
A glimpse of a time without constant sorrow
Time is relentless, time is pain

Nature's Breath

The winds scream through the trees
I want to scream back
But the wind of my chest will not
Match natures breath
I fall and hit the earth beneath me
The gods frown down upon me from the ether above
beyond what thy eyes can see
But thou return a smile that shuns their gaze

YOU MIGHT FEEL THIS

Stormy Nights

Stormy nights, midnight frights
My eyes closed tight from seeing the moon's lights
The plain is cold and alone
As am I laid to this stone
The throne I gaze upon is empty
As is thy heart for thee
Shush the howling winds
They have become too loud
I can no longer hear your voice
Please shout so I can hear thee
Or has your flame gone out
Please, please, don't leave thee here
I can feel your presence is near
One more climb, one more calm
Upon the ruckus sea
That is where you will find thee
Alone until dust and bone
The winter brings death
Flowers on graves dead like the bone beneath them

Your thoughts here

Forgo The Sun

I will forgo the sun, as long as I have the moon
Its pale light shines through the trees
Waking the skeletons of the past from their graves
The witches laughter smothers the sound of the wolf's howl
The cauldron makes something my mortal soul can not taste
It is a taste of joy the taste of things not seen
A stone moves in front of me
It leaves a void into the depths of change
May I enter? I scream into this hollowness
This dark empty nothingness
My voice travels far as men do to the seas. My voice did not
return to me just as shipwrecked men to the shores

Your thoughts here

Distant Traveler

Humble and distant traveler
Where have you gone?
What have you seen?
Might I tell the tale of my adventure
To the grand realm of no pain nor suffering
It is beautiful and free of chains and harsh tongues. No
longer do their words cut into the flesh as a sharp blade.
The blood does not flow as harshly as a belligerent river
For I have seen this land with my own eyes and ever curious mind.
Gates of prosperity and knowledge await. To
those who embrace cultivation

Your thoughts here

Trepidation

All is once again mine
All that I have lost has been returned
I live for this feeling
For the ones, you can only feel
But not fully understand
The moments without the crippling anxiety
and fear is swept away
My brain is clear as a blue spring sky
May I keep this sealed up tight in a bottle? This bottle
harbors a ship
I wish this ship could sail
Sail far across the sea of tranquillity
For it shall reach others who have been trapped
under the forceful thumb of anxiety
Or, shall I put this monster disguised as fear into this bottle?
Send it out aboard the ship?
I wish for a peaceful storm to take hold of
this ship named trepidation
The tide shall take away the vulnerable port of disquiet
Tide, merciful, tide. Please, be on our side.

YOU MIGHT FEEL THIS

Your thoughts here

Death's Mask

Heads no longer bow as I walk by
Faces no longer smile in my presence
They are replaced by a death mask
A pure empty void of emotion
The past has lied to me
It has told me a false fable
Do not fear the night
For the night does not fear itself
The present keeps me in the dark
Though I love to be in the shadows
I do look for warmth given by the sun
Or the comfort of your skin
Your love is indifferent

Your thoughts here

The Fire's Blaze

The fires blaze, swallowing everything in their path
The waters of compassion can suppress them
I need you now I need your calm and soothing wave
For I have seen this
In my dreams of unforgiving fire
The unrelenting pain has ceased
For the fires are now gone
I am now engulfed by your beauty
My fair maiden for whom I love
With all of my heart
Your love gives me vigorous strength
Strength I have not found bottled
Nor manufactured

Your thoughts here

They Throw Stones

My name is upheld in the ballads of men and women.
I fear I am losing their confidence
I press my hand into the rained
ground below me.
My hand feels its cold but soothing comfort
I see my reflection and I have to ponder.
Is this truly what I have become?
Is this the person they see while gazing upon my aging face?
Why must the world spin so slowly for me but
move at such a fast pace for others?
Am I not worthy of the care and affection others receive at their bedside while ill Will the thunderstorm sound more magnificent to more worthy ears? Alas, I can no longer continue this painful charade. I dawn a new disguise making my way through streets I called home. No one throws parades any longer for me, only stones.

Your thoughts here

Soul's Robbery

This world is my creation
I can no longer dwell here.
A robbery of my soul has been committed
For too long have I only just existed
The skeleton of civilization is apparent
For this land now feels like a prison
A torture hollowed echo chamber of anguish.
I follow bread crumbs to the cemetery gates
The ghost of you guards them
Will you invite me in?

YOU MIGHT FEEL THIS

Your thoughts here

Immortality's Truth

The rain patters against my window
As if it were trying to ask for an invitation into my hollow room
Why must I be attached to this mortal flesh of a body?
Why can I not be free as the rain is from a cloud?
I feel trapped and anchored to this chair
As I breathe such shallow breaths
Each breath gives away what little life I have left to give
I want to be selfish
I want to breathe forever
I know I will one day be one with the ground below my feet
But this is not the venture I wish to explore before
I find my truth in immortality

Your thoughts here

FOREVER IS COMPOSED OF NOWS

-Emily Dickinson

Made in the USA
Columbia, SC
05 January 2022